My dearest
friend,

all my fondest
love

To:

_____

From:

_____

ISBN: 0-88396-949-1

Certain trademarks are used under license.

Manufactured in China.
First Printing: 2005

✪ This book is printed on recycled paper.

Blue Mountain Arts, Inc.
P.O. Box 4549, Boulder, Colorado 80306

A Little Bit of…

GOD
in Every Day

Blue Mountain Arts®

Boulder, Colorado

God Holds
You Close
to His
Heart

May your heart find peace
and comfort in the knowledge
that you are never alone.
May God's presence ease
your spirit
    and give you rest.
He knows how you feel…

He is ever aware of your
   circumstances
and ready to be
your strength, your grace,
and your peace.
He is there to cast
sunlight into all your
   darkened shadows.

He sends encouragement
through the love of friends
and family,
and replaces your weariness
with new hope.
He is your stronghold;
with Him as your guide,
you need never be afraid…

No circumstances can block
    God's love.
No grief is too hard for Him
    to bear.
No task is too difficult
for Him to complete.

When what you are feeling
is simply too deep for words,
God understands.
He is your provider —
today, tomorrow, and always.
And He loves you.
Cast all your cares on Him…
and believe.

— Linda E. Knight

Have Faith

Faith isn't anything
you can see or touch;
you feel it in your heart.
It keeps you trying when
others have given up.
It keeps you believing in
the goodness of others
and helps you find it...

Faith is trusting in a power
greater than yourself
and knowing this power will
carry you through anything.
It is believing in yourself
and having the courage
to stand up for what you
believe in.

Faith is peace
in the midst of a storm,
determination in the midst
of adversity,
and safety in the midst
of trouble.
For nothing can touch
a soul protected by faith.

— Barbara Cage

Anything
Is Possible
Because of
God

It is God who enables you
to smile in spite of tears;
to carry on when you
    feel like giving in;
to pray when you're at a
    loss for words…

It is God who enables you
to love even though
    your heart has been
broken time and time again;
to sit calmly when you feel
like throwing up your hands
in frustration;

to be understanding when
nothing seems to make sense;
to share your feelings
   with others,
because sharing is necessary
   to ease the load.
Anything is possible,
because God makes it so.

— Faye Sweeney

God Knows
What You're
Going
Through

When you are tired
and discouraged from
    fruitless efforts,
God knows how hard you
    have tried.
When you've cried so long
and your heart's in anguish,
God has counted
    your tears...

If you feel your life
    is on hold,
and time has passed you by,
God is waiting with you.
When you're lonely
and your friends are too
busy even for a phone call,
God is by your side.

When you think you've
tried everything,
and don't know where to
turn, God has a solution.
When nothing makes sense
and you are confused
or frustrated…
God has the answer…

When things are going well
and you have much to be
thankful for,
God has blessed you.
When something joyful
    happens
and you are filled with awe,
God has smiled upon you.

When you have a purpose
to fulfill
and a dream to follow,
God has opened your eyes
and called you by name.
Wherever you are
or whatever you're facing…
God knows.

— Kelly D. Williams

You are not alone. You never have been, and you never will be. God has been with you every step of the way. Where the path leads, He is lighting lamps to guide you.

If you ever do feel He is not right there beside you, it's only because He has gone ahead to build a bridge to keep you safe from harm and lead you toward the sunlight shining through.

— Alin Austin

God isn't far away.
He is the light of this day.
He is the sky above you,
the earth beneath you,
and the life of every
living thing.

He is in every smile,
in every thought that
gives you hope,
in every tear that
waters your soul,
and in every moment
you can't face alone...

God is the love on your
loved one's face.
He's in the friends
along the way —
in strangers you have
yet to meet
and blessings you have
yet to receive.

He's in every good thing
that touches you.
He is in every step you make
and every breath you take.
He's not far away,
for He is with you always.

— Nancye Sims

God has a thousand ways
Where I can see not one;
When all my means have
reached their end
Then His have just begun.

— Esther Guyot

God shall be my hope,
My stay, my guide and
lantern to my feet.

— William Shakespeare

When One
Door Closes
God Opens
Another

Sometimes when we
least expect it,
a door closes in our lives.
Circumstances may change,
dreams may get shattered,
and plans for tomorrow
may disappear.
But when one door closes,
God always opens another…

When we're facing
disappointment in our lives,
sometimes it's hard to see
that this is also part
    of God's plan —
but it's true.
God knows what is best
    for us.

He will lead you
to where you need to be.
Have faith in Him,
and you will reach
all the wondrous things
He has waiting for you.

— B. L. McDaniel

God hath not promised
Skies always blue,
Flower-strewn pathways
All our lives through;
God hath not promised
Sun without rain,
Joy without sorrow,
Peace without pain.

But God hath promised
Strength for the day,
Rest for the labor,
Light for the way,
Grace for the trials,
Help from above,
Unfailing sympathy,
Undying love.

— Annie Johnson Flint

Remember
What It Means
to Have
the Lord
in Your Life

Having the Lord in your
life means you have peace
and comfort in your heart
as you walk down any
pathway your life has
to offer...

It means you can pray to a caring and compassionate Father who always has the time to listen and never fails to understand the hurts and fears dwelling in the depths of your soul.

Having the Lord in your life means having the assurance that nothing can ever come your way that you and He, united together, cannot deal with and ultimately overcome.

— Cathy Beddow Keener

Sometimes life sends us
changes we've never
   contemplated,
problems we'd just as soon
   do without,
and inconveniences we'd
rather not have to
deal with.

It can feel as if we are wandering in a barren desert. It's during these "desert" experiences of our lives that God, in all

His faithfulness,

opens up His heart…

God quenches our
    thirsty souls,
revives our parched hearts,
and leads us to
    a higher place
where peace, joy, and love
    will be ours forever.

On all the long journeys
your life leads you on,
please remember...

you'll never walk alone.

— Linda E. Knight

You
Are
Blessed

You are blessed...
if your soul has faith,
and your faith in God
   is strong,
if, even when your heart
   is aching,
it can still sing
an uplifting song...

You are blessed...
if you find contentment
in life's simple,
   priceless joys;
if you have a quiet spot
to retreat from
all the world's noise;

if you're embraced with love
by family, friends,
    and others;
if you feel you're one
with your world of
    sisters and brothers...

If you can give a hug
to those who need it most;
if you can show the lonely
that your heart is a
welcoming host;

if your hopes are high
and you keep
your dreams alive;
if you don't think
    you'll quit,
but persist and strive...
You are blessed.

— Jacqueline Schiff

*Someone's
Watching
Over You*

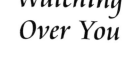

Someone's watching over
you with the greatest love.
Someone wants you to be
happy, safe, and secure;
Someone considers you
a wonderful individual
and cares about
your needs…

Someone's making blessings
for your benefit
right now —
like sunshine for those
rainy days
and rainbows to remind you
of the promise up ahead.

Someone's watching over
you today and always…
And He will take
good care of you.

— Barbara J. Hall